T0029816

DOROTHY
THE BRAVE

Meghan P. Browne

Illustrated by Brooke Smart

VIKING

Warm milk sung in the pail.
Squee-squirt. Squee-squirt.
Dorothy dreamed of a thousand places she'd rather be than
fetching milk and eggs in middle-of-nowhere North Carolina.

During the Great Depression, farmers weren't the only folks raising
animals and tending crops. With her daddy gone, and following two
older brothers and a big sister, Dorothy quickly learned to do her part
to survive. Even after all these years and moving too many times,
she could hardly wait to leave this life behind.

The day petals fell from the tulip tree, Mother asked Dorothy
to pack a bag. Time had come to leave the Lonesome Valley,
but she hadn't expected to go it alone.

Dorothy did the bravest thing she could. It excited her a little.
It scared her, too. She boarded a train to Aunt Georgie and
Uncle Melvin's in Washington, DC . . .

Dorothy danced the jitterbug and earned her high school diploma in the city. She ate pineapple ice cream in the soda parlor and swam in the salty Atlantic. Out across the waves, on the distant shore of that wide ocean, things were terribly wrong.

One Sunday afternoon in early December, Dorothy reunited with her oldest brother, Mason, and Mother over peanuts and popcorn for a football game at Griffith Stadium. A crackling loudspeaker interrupted play on the field, commanding a navy admiral to report to his office at once.

Dorothy looked to Mother, confused. The booming voice came again and again, summoning generals, politicians, and intelligence agents. The autumn air electrified. People rose from their seats. Dorothy turned to ask what in the world it could mean.

"Nothing good," Mason said.

Far out west past the coast of California, the sun was only just peeking over the vast Pacific Ocean. Whistling bombs fell from the bellies of enemy aircraft, splitting the silence at dawn. Civilians and sailors at Pearl Harbor just like Dorothy's brother, Courtland, woke to a fiery nightmare.

The next day, newspapers screamed in bold block: WAR!

All of those officials who raced from the game the night before had done their duty of declaration. A spark ignited inside of Dorothy as she asked the same question every American wondered: *What will I do to help?*

Dorothy's brothers shipped out: Courtland sailed rough seas aboard a Navy battleship. Mason read maps and worked calculations while navigating the skies over the Atlantic.

Dorothy reported for duty, too. She spent her wartime days as a Pentagon clerk handling secret documents and her nights taking college courses. From bustling cities to windswept farm towns, men marched off to war, and women who had been mothers, secretaries, and teachers took up new work.

They riveted like Rosie.

They nursed like Kate.

ROSIE THE RIVETER,
INDUSTRIAL WORKER

KATE NOLAN,
COMBAT NURSE

They clerked like Dorothy.

Somewhere in the very root of her being, Dorothy grew determined to do even more for her country. Something as important as her brothers' work. Something impossible. Something that excited her a lot and scared her, too.

A friend whispered from behind her desk one morning—
a new outfit was recruiting experienced pilots.

They transported planes over amber waves of grain and above
purple mountain majesties.

They towed targets high in the air followed by brand-new airmen
whose gunnery crews learned to shoot enemy planes out of the sky.

And all of the pilots were—impossibly—women.

In order to apply, Dorothy would first have to learn to fly.
Many others who had proven themselves were daughters of wealth.
Their families could afford flying lessons even during that great
hard time before the war. Dorothy didn't know that kind of luxury,
but she didn't mind making her own luck, either. She gathered
her courage and asked Mother for a loan to pay for lessons.
Two hundred dollars—the kind of money that could put a roof
over your head for months, but Mother never hesitated in handing
over her savings.

Dorothy took flight, knowing that Mother had given her wings.

Thirty-five hours of roaring engines.
Thirty-five hours of defying gravity.
Thirty-five hours of feeling the airplane respond to her touch.

She had never felt so in control. Racing on the wind behind the switches and knobs of a tiny crop duster, Dorothy found her bravest, truest self.

With her very own pilot's license in hand, Dorothy wasted no time applying to the WASP (Women Airforce Service Pilots) program. There was still much yet to prove, but Dorothy didn't mind.

As soon as they passed their interviews, Dorothy and two other eager applicants climbed inside a brand-new convertible and watched the east coast disappear in the rearview mirror. Fifteen hundred miles later, the trio of pioneers pulled into a railroad town named Sweetwater, where months of rigorous training spread out before them like a snowy sea of cotton on the West Texas prairie.

COLORADO

KANSAS

MISSOURI

NEW MEXICO

SWEETWATER

OKLAHOMA

ARKANSAS

TEXAS

LOUISIANA

MISSISS

VERMONT

WISCONSIN

MICHIGAN

NEW YORK

MASSA-

WASHINGTON DC

PENNSYLVANIA

NEW JERSEY

DELAWARE

MARYLAND

OHIO

INDIANA

NOIS

WEST VIRGINIA

VIRGINIA

KENTUCKY

NORTH CAROLINA

TENNESSEE

SOUTH CAROLINA

ALABAMA

GEORGIA

FLORIDA

Spring in the panhandle brought hot, dry days that could turn in an instant when gullywashers rode in on thunderclouds so tall they seemed ready to swallow any airborne creature whole. In summer, the air might as well have poured from an oven, and the women carried their beds outside the stifling barracks to sleep beneath a blanket of stars.

Dorothy and her classmates had to prove they were brave enough, strong enough, daring enough—or pay their own way home.

As dawn broke over Avenger Field the day of Dorothy's solo flight, the morning breeze blew across the plains and called her up into the skies. She would finally prove herself worthy of wearing the wings of the WASP by handling her aircraft with grace and grit.

Way out over miles and miles of wire, a telegram came dotting and dashing its way to Sweetwater. Mother's words on that paper rectangle cracked Dorothy wide open.

Mason had died in an aviation accident. Mother, who had always given Dorothy plenty of room to stretch her wings wide, now called her home.

A small, terrible voice inside Dorothy grew loud, begging to know why a simple girl thought she could make a difference in this huge, horrible war.

WESTERN UNION

AVENGER FIELD = SWEETWATER TX

DEAREST DOT

MASON DIED COME HOME=

MOTHER.

Dorothy's classmates found her packing for home, but they couldn't let her leave. She had come too far—they all had—not to see this through. In the sisterhood of her fellow fly girls, she found the courage to continue. Dorothy would do her part to put an end to this awful war. She would direct her aircraft skyward again.

Dorothy received her first assignment and prepared for takeoff. She climbed to the clouds and checked her mirrors for the banner streaming behind. The sky buzzed with brand-new fighter pilots and their freshly minted gunnery crews training to liberate Europe. Round after round of live ammunition thundered over the drone of her engine and peppered the target attached to Dorothy's tail. Stray bullets bit through her plane, stealing Dorothy's breath. She missed Mother, and home, and Dorothy wondered if that was where she belonged.

Dorothy forced herself to keep her wits.

Steady on, Dot. They're not aiming at you, she reminded herself.

The gunnery squadron flew alongside her, preparing for their approach back to base. Those boys with their kind eyes and their wide grins—just like her brothers'—needed Dorothy's courage as much as the country needed them. Dorothy took one more pass riding the wind before steering herself home.

★ ★ AUTHOR'S NOTE ★ ★

The Women Airforce Service Pilots (WASP) organization was born out of a merger between the Women's Flying Training Detachment (WFTD), led by Jacqueline Cochran, and the Women's Auxiliary Ferrying Squadron (WAFS), led by Nancy Love. Cochran and Love, two of the most noteworthy female disrupters of the twentieth century, leveraged intelligence and hard work to curate a trail-

Dorothy Ann Smith Lucas (top row, far right) and fellow WASP 44-W-7 classmates in Sweetwater, Texas.

blazing group of women who would change the face of aviation forever.

Twenty-five thousand young women from cities and towns across the country applied, and 1,830 were accepted as trainees. Dorothy Ann Smith Lucas, an independent young woman from Virginia, was one of only 1,074 pilots to complete the training required by the WASP. When Dorothy's training in Sweetwater came to an end, she was sent to Moore Field in Mission, Texas, where she predominantly towed targets for the gunnery squadron there.

The WASP were trained for domestic aviation duties at home to free up men for combat missions abroad. Despite some female European and Russian pilots flying combat missions during World War II, it would be an-

Dorothy, WASP-in-training.

other half century before female pilots in the United States Air Force were allowed to hold combat roles.

Dorothy Ann Smith Lucas, WASP graduate, Class 44-W-7.

Dorothy and her silver-winged WASP sisters collectively logged more than sixty million miles in every kind of aircraft in military service at the time but were not recognized as members of the United States military. Due to this lapse in recognition, when a WASP lost her life on the line, her classmates and friends would often pass a hat to help raise the funds needed to transport her remains back home. Thirty-eight WASP died serving.

Like other aspects of American life in the 1940s, the WASP organization was not immune to racial discrimination. The organization saw only five women of color graduate with silver wings: Frances Dias (Mexican American), Maggie Gee (Chinese American), Ola Mildred Rexroat (Oglala Sioux), Verneda Rodriguez (Mexican American), and Hazel Ying Lee (Chinese American). Many African American women applied for admission to the WASP training program, but none made it past the final interview stage, including Mildred Hemmons Carter, who was recognized retroactively as both a WASP and an honorary member of the Tuskegee Airmen.

The disbanding of the WASP came in late December of 1944, prior to the end of World War II, under political and social pressure amid concern that the WASP were taking jobs from their male counterparts.

In 1977, thirty-three years after Dorothy's solo flight, President Jimmy Carter awarded the WASP veteran status following a bicameral congressional effort led by Senator Barry Goldwater (R-AZ). On March 10, 2010, sixty-six years after they were disbanded, following a push from an all-female delegation—Senators Kay Bailey Hutchison (R-TX) and Barbara Mikulski (D-MD) and Representatives Ileana Ros-Lehtinen (R-FL) and Susan Davis (D-CA)—President Barack Obama awarded the WASP the Congressional Gold Medal. Dorothy's motivation to serve her country in such an unorthodox way was simple: She wanted to do her part. The spirit of independence that her mother fostered in Dorothy allowed her to believe that her call to service was different than nursing, teaching, boarding a navy ship as a clerk, or riveting. Dorothy's place was in the sky. Once she had her silver wings, Dorothy never doubted again in her life that she could accomplish the things she set out to complete.

Dorothy at the controls in the cockpit.

On Memorial Day weekend 2018, I followed Dorothy to an annual WASP homecoming at Avenger Field in Sweetwater. At ninety-five years old, Dorothy was one of four WASP well enough to travel to the event. I watched her graciously sign an endless stream of autographs with her left hand, but Dorothy hadn't been a southpaw long. Dorothy became a lefty after suffering a stroke late in life, and undeterred, she re-taught herself to write.

The same woman who bucked rigid gender roles in the 1940s is the same woman who, many decades later, still sees obstacles as doors through which to pass . . . bravely.

Dorothy (top row, second from right) with her fellow WASP at Avenger Field.

Dorothy directed skyward.

RECOMMENDED READING

★ *A WASP Among Eagles: A Woman Military Test Pilot in World War II* by Ann B. Carl

★ *At the Mountain's Base* by Traci Sorell

★ *Sky High: The True Story of Maggie Gee* by Marissa Moss

★ *The Fearless Flights of Hazel Ying Lee* by Julie Leung

★ *Fly Girls: The Daring American Women Pilots Who Helped Win WWII*

    by P. O'Connell Pearson

★ *Nancy Love and the WASP Ferry Pilots of World War II* by Sarah Byrn Rickman

★ *Skyward* by Sally Deng

★ *WASP of the Ferry Command: Women Pilots, Uncommon Deeds*

    by Sarah Byrn Rickman

★ *WASPs: Women Airforce Service Pilots of World War II* by Vera S. Williams

For Dorothy and her WASP sisters,
who blazed a skyward trail most valiantly.
—M. P. B.

For my sisters, mother, and grandmothers.
Thanks for teaching me how to be brave.
—B. S.

VIKING

An imprint of Penguin Random House LLC, New York

First published in the United States of America by Viking,
an imprint of Penguin Random House LLC, 2022

Text copyright © 2022 by Meghan P. Browne
Illustrations copyright © 2022 by Brooke Smart

Penguin supports copyright. Copyright fuels creativity, encourages diverse voices,
promotes free speech, and creates a vibrant culture. Thank you for buying an authorized edition
of this book and for complying with copyright laws by not reproducing, scanning, or distributing
any part of it in any form without permission. You are supporting writers and allowing Penguin
to continue to publish books for every reader.

Viking & colophon are registered trademarks of Penguin Random House LLC.

Visit us online at penguinrandomhouse.com.

Library of Congress Cataloging-in-Publication Data is available.

Manufactured in China

ISBN 9780593116999

10 9 8 7 6 5 4 3 2 1

TOPL

All photos courtesy of the Lucas family.
Design by Opal Roengchai
Text set in New Caledonia LT Std
The illustrations were created in gouache, watercolor, and colored pencil.

This is a work of nonfiction. Some names and identifying details have been changed.

The publisher does not have any control over and does not assume any responsibility
for author or third-party websites or their content.